Collecting Louis `

Paul Pluta

Revision 10

www.collectinglouisvuitton.com

Free updates for this book available at

www.collectinglouisvuitton.com/updates.html

Email – hiromi_kirishima@yahoo.com

ISBN 978-1-4461-6949-0